Why Are You Worrying?

Joseph W. Ciarrocchi

Paulist Press
New York/Mahwah, New Jersey

Cover/book design and interior illustrations by Nicholas T. Markell.

Library of Congress Cataloging-in-Publication Data

Ciarrocchi, Joseph W.
    Why are you worrying? / Joseph W. Ciarrocchi.
        p.   cm.—(IlluminationBooks)
    Includes bibliographical references (p.).
    ISBN 0-8091-3561-2
    1. Worry—Religious aspects—Christianity. I. Title. II. Series.
BV4908.5C43   1995
248.8´6—dc20   95-3039
                                                                CIP

Published by Paulist Press
997 Macarthur Boulevard
Mahwah, New Jersey 07430

Printed and bound in the
United States of America

Contents

Dedication

To Robert Sullivan.
Poet, culture-worrier, and friend.

Acknowledgments

The Pastoral Counseling department of Loyola College in Maryland provides continuous support as an academic and faith community. Bob Wicks brought up the idea for this book during a ten minute class break when I was picking up mail and messages. Only halfway into the next lecture did I appreciate what I had accepted.

Sister Shirley Peace, OSF helped me worry less through her capable ministry as my graduate assistant. She collected sources and formatted the figures.

Again I thank my children Michael, Laura, Katie, Jennifer and Daniel for the love they provide me during our own worrisome times. Jennifer (age 8), when hearing what Dad was writing on the computer, confronted me with the fact that a worry book is needed for children, "Because they feel safe and secure if they don't learn to take chances." Perhaps that will be a future project.

IlluminationBooks

A Foreword

*I*lluminationBooks bring to light wonderful
ideas, helpful information, and sound
spirituality in concise, illustrative, read-
able, and eminently practical works on topics of
current concern. Learning from stress; interior
peace; personal prayer; biblical awareness; walking
with others in darkness; appreciating the love
already in our lives; spiritual discernment; uncover-
ing helpful psychological antidotes for our tendency
to worry too much at times; and important guides
to improving interpersonal relations, are only several of the areas which will be covered in this series.

The goal of each IlluminationBook, then, is to provide great ideas, helpful steps, and needed inspiration in small volumes. Each book offers a new beginning for the reader to explore possibilities and embrace practicalities which can be employed in everyday life.

In today's busy and anxious world, Illumination-Books are meant to provide a source of support—without requiring an inordinate amount of time or prior preparation. Each small work stands on its own. Hopefully, the information provided not only will be nourishing in itself but also will encourage further exploration in the area.

One is obviously never done learning. With every morsel of wisdom each of these books provides, the goal is to keep the process of seeking knowledge ongoing even during busy times, when sitting down with a larger work is impossible or undesirable.

However, more than information (as valuable as it is), at the base of each work in the series is a deep sense of *hope* that is based on a belief in the beautiful statement made by Jesus to his disciples and in turn to us: "You are my friends" (Jn 15:15).

As "friends of God" we must seek the presence of the Lord in ourselves, in others, in silence and solitude, in nature, and in daily situations. IlluminationBooks are designed to provide implicit and explicit opportunities to appreciate this reality in new ways. So, it is in this spirit that this book and the other ones in the series are offered to you.   –*Robert J. Wicks*

General Editor, IlluminationBooks

Introduction
Worry and the Soul

"*I* should like you not to worry."
1 Corinthians 7:32

Worry and fear are so much a part of life that our sacred writings speak about them often. The spiritual antidote to fear and worry seems to be wisdom. "[With Wisdom] Then you may securely go your way; your foot will never stumble; when you lie down, you need not be afraid, when you rest, your sleep will be sweet" (Proverbs 3:24).

But this wisdom is a curious thing. The biblical meaning is surely not mere intellectual knowledge. In fact, many warnings are given to the pretentious and puffed-up. Rather, wisdom is God's wisdom, a gift we

are to seek. When Solomon asks this gift of God, he pleases God.

A second curious feature about wisdom is its relationship to fear; that is, fear of the Lord. Repeatedly scripture points out the importance of having this fear. This notion annoys our modern mind; a mind-set that desires to emphasize the softer qualities of the Creator—love, understanding and mercy. But we cannot progress in wisdom if we avoid the paradoxes of belief. The scriptures describe fear of the Lord in sweet terms and point to the serenity it brings.

This holy paradox, this relationship between facing fear and the serenity it brings, is the core to achieving a measure of freedom from worry. In this book I explore this relationship in two ways. First I will describe the exciting discoveries about anxiety and worry in modern psychology. Second, I will attempt to integrate these findings within the perspective of religious belief. I maintain that *freedom from excessive worry and fear is enhanced by having a religious or spiritual perspective.*

The premise of an IlluminationBook requires that this book be brief. I can only provide a sketchy road map, but, I believe, an accurate one based on the latest research on anxiety. What is innovative is the integration of spirituality with these methods. The spiritual ideas invoked, however, are certainly not new, and may be quite familiar or even routine to you. What this road map suggests is pathways to make you more *aware* of your spiritual insights, and to apply them in a *systematic* fashion. Anxiety impedes performance. Even spiritual performance. If this little volume serves only to refocus you on the depths within and without, it will have succeeded.

Chapter One

Worry: Definitions and Impact

"*If we submit everything to reason, our religion will have nothing in it mysterious or supernatural. If we violate the principles of reason, our religion will be absurd and ridiculous.*"

–Blaise Pascal

The experience of worry

Worry is a future-directed anxiety, discomfort about possible or inevitable negative events. When you worry you experience one or all of the following. You may feel a sense of apprehension that something bad could happen which forces you to keep vigilant to prevent it. Even though the event is *unpredictable*, you still have to be on

guard. Not only is it unpredictable, but you sense that it is *uncontrollable* as well. When something is both unpredictable *and* uncontrollable you must be especially vigilant.

Your worry often has an **internal physical** component. You may notice your stomach churning, a choking sensation in your throat, sweating, headaches, dizziness, a racing heart, difficulty breathing, or pains in your chest. You may even seek medical treatment for these symptoms.

Worrying has an **external behavioral** component. You may shake or be jittery. You may pace back and forth, have difficulty concentrating, check to see if you have done things correctly more than is necessary. Or, you may procrastinate or avoid doing essential tasks. Worry may trigger in you a desire to escape, to get away from it all, to not even look at the problem (for example, paying your bills).

Another unpleasant feature of worry is that it makes you **self-conscious**. Your behavior may start to resemble a character in a Woody Allen movie. You become aware of every movement, judging each step as to its correctness. You may start to think, "Am I doing this right? Is anyone noticing that I'm upset? How do I look? I'm sure I'm goofing this up." You may even start to feel like a fraud. "How long can I keep fooling people till they find out how incompetent I am?"

The effects of worry

Excessive worry interferes with your performance. Paying attention to all the internal noise that goes along with worry means that you are less effective with the task at hand. Effective performance requires a balance between too little concern and too much. If you don't care about a task (e.g., an upcoming examination) you might not give it enough effort. Too much concern may result in freezing on the test questions even if you know the answers.

The internal noise and self-consciousness of worry may even interfere with your relationships. You may have a great capacity for giving, yet because of your self-consciousness may give others *the exact opposite impression*. You may notice an interesting person at a social gathering, but your preoccupation about each move leaves you standing by yourself, or not venturing beyond old friends.

For some the constant stirring of adverse physical sensations leads to physical ailments. Stress-related disorders are common for worriers: gastrointestinal problems, rashes, tension headaches, to name a few. You may notice that you turn to self-defeating coping strategies when worry starts to get to you. These may include overeating, drinking excessive amounts of alcohol, or using medications in a non-prescribed manner. Before long, excessive worrying demoralizes you. You may end up believing your situation is hopeless and you are helpless to change it. You may be unable to shake what used to be momentary depression.

Worry also demoralizes your spiritual well-being. Your joy in faith departs. Now your main task is avoiding failure. You stop risking, stretching yourself, trying new ventures. God no longer walks with you as a support. Rather, you are likely to perceive God as the Judge, or

Evaluator. This state now resembles fear of the Lord in the frightening, non-biblical sense.

Normal versus abnormal worry

You can essentially worry about anything. Typically, however, about 85% of ordinary worries involve finances, health or safety issues, family problems, relationships, work or occupation. Surveys show that practically everyone worries about these themes. What moves a worry from normal to abnormal?

Although it is hazardous to label any behavior abnormal, worry is even more complicated. You may feel that your worry is justified. After all, if you are concerned about having cancer, it's *your* life, and who can tell you worrying is not justified? Worry themes become abnormal if you give too much time to a specific worry, or if your concern is over an event that has little chance of happening.

You may even feel that you can no longer determine whether your worrying is excessive. Now **worrying seems like a plausible way to handle your problem**. In other words, you feel pulled to the worrying *process* itself, even if you find the worry *content* unpleasant and disagreeable. One way to determine if your worrying is excessive is to see how it affects your life. Are your worries interfering with your occupation, concentration, sleeping, or your health? Have you put off essential tasks because of worrying? Does the quality of your life suffer significantly because you avoid potentially enjoyable activities or chances to meet people?

I hope this book will help you whether your worries are either run-of-the-mill, ordinary worries or excessive. I am not addressing some types of anxiety problems here. **Panic attacks** involve a sudden upsurge in intense fear that seems to come out of nowhere. A person with this problem begins to worry all the time about having a panic attack. This book will not deal with eliminating fear of panic attacks. However, people with panic attacks are often chronic worriers as well, so they may find some relief with the strategies in this book.

Post-traumatic stress involves worry generated from previous trauma (e.g., physical or sexual assault, natural catastrophes, war experience, etc.). The person worries about events or situations that trigger these unpleasant memories. **Obsessive-compulsive disorder** triggers worries related to obsessions or compulsions. Obsessions are difficult-to-shake thoughts, urges, impulses, or ideas that trigger anxiety and which are usually repulsive to the person. Obsessions may relate to excessive concerns about safety, disease, aggressive impulses, blasphemous ideas or sexual matters. They usually are accompanied by compulsions.

Compulsions are repeated acts, thoughts or ideas that neutralize the anxiety associated with an obsession. For example, people wash their hands excessively because of fear of germs; others check door and window locks repeatedly over safety concerns. Unlike the content of general worry, the content of obsessions is quite repugnant (e.g., blasphemous or sexually inappropriate matters).

Finally, worries associated with **controlling one's**

impulses represent another area not addressed here. These include urges to abuse alcohol, drugs, to gamble excessively, act aggressively, or engage in sexual misconduct. Persons with these problems need to obtain information specifically directed to those issues. Again, however, many persons with these problems also are chronic worriers. Sometimes they use their impulsive behavior to obtain relief from other worries. If you fit this pattern, you may find the strategies in this book beneficial.

Chapter Two
The Worry Cycle

Y ou worry with good reason. The capacity to worry separates you from animals. One psychologist calls worry "the shadow of intelligence," for it represents one aspect of your ability to plan and think. The tendency to worry is adaptive. Crickets have little concern about nuclear waste, the depletion of the ozone, or alterations in the global food-chain cycle. Yet crickets have as much at stake in solving these problems as humans. Lack of concern for these issues would result in planetary disasters.

The same holds for personal worries. Without

concern for the future you would not hold a job, organize into social groups to meet your needs, use money to obtain food, or find suitable housing.

Adaptive worry, therefore, functions as a *problem-solving mechanism*. Excessive worry, however, has lost this problem-solving feature. When you worry excessively you *believe* you are problem-solving, but in reality you are spinning your wheels in a fruitless, unending preoccupation. Excessive worry, then, is a trick that thinking and feeling play. The alarm goes off that you have a problem (anxiety). Then your mental apparatus kicks into gear to try to solve it (thinking or cognition). But you cannot solve the problem because your fear becomes excessive and interferes with rational solutions.

Let's imagine that over the next two or three months you will face financial difficulties. As you are trying to fall asleep at night your thoughts take the following course. Note that each ^ mark indicates an idea that increases your anxiety further.

> The rent is due in five days [^]. I have just enough to cover it. But, there's also the bank credit card; I can't possibly cover that [^]. Maybe I could borrow from my parents. I forgot about the money I owe on the doctor bill [^]. I have to go back for my follow-up visit, and that will be embarrassing if I can't pay it off [^]. Well, maybe I could put the visit off a couple of weeks. Oh, no, I forgot Susie needs a winter coat; she out-

grew her old one [^]. She will be *so* disappointed if I have to put that off, or if we have to get it at the second-hand shop [^].

This example illustrates how the worry cycle changes into the worry spiral. Nature intends that worry generate solutions to problems. When you focus only on the potential threats and dangers, worry spirals out of control.

Anatomy of the worry spiral

To be simplistic, maladaptive reactions to worry can take one of two forms. Some focus on feeling helpless, convinced that terrible things will happen. They imagine there is little they can do to prevent the negative event, yet they feel they *must* keep worrying about it. Others react in the opposite direction. They dwell on their skills and a "can-do" attitude. They pour energy into external activities rather than mental ones. Their extreme belief in being able to control events often results in a state of annoyance, irritation and flashes of hostility. These "Type A" persons often ignore their body's physical early-warning signs because of their intense external focus. As a result, they are more prone to stress-related or cardiovascular illness than others.

Either reaction of excessive undercontrol or over-control, therefore, has negative effects. As the Greek philosophers reminded us centuries ago, "Virtue stands in the middle." Dwelling on helplessness intensifies fear and makes effective action unlikely; dwelling on control blinds one to the realistic acceptance of events beyond human control.

Since I am concerned mostly with the worries that come from a sense of undercontrol, the anatomy of this spiral bears examining. When you fall into the worry spiral your constant attention to the dangers around you (hypervigilance), leads to *overpredicting the likelihood of the negative event.* If you are worried about crime in your neighborhood, you will interpret every noise, the appearance of each stranger, the existence of any rumor as proof that criminal activity is happening all around you. Research shows, for example, that if you watch television frequently, you are likely to have an exaggerated belief in the amount and frequency of crime. Consequently you may restrict your life unnecessarily and become a shut-in because of unrealistic worry.

The second mechanism that maintains the worry spiral involves *catastrophizing.* Not only does worry lead to predicting the immediacy of a negative event, but further leads you to predict, "*I cannot handle it if it does arrive.*" It is one thing to lose your job and predict that it would be an inconvenience and a major hassle. It is something different to see yourself as never recovering and standing in a food line for the rest of your life. Catastrophizing subverts the natural problem-solving component to the worry cycle. It raises anxiety to such a level that you can only focus on the unmanageability of the event. Both overpredicting and catastrophizing create worry through your imagination.

Anxiety fires up when your brain and body take your negative view of the situation and run with it.

Worry and the fear that accompanies it makes you forget for the moment the hundreds of times you managed difficulties, overcame crises, or coped with stressors. This "selective amnesia" fuels your view that the situation is unmanageable. Your inner dialogue changes from, "This will be a pain to deal with, but I have been through worse and can pull this off," to, "This is terrible and awful and I just can't deal with it."

For some the worry spiral is so automatic that anything different feels unnatural. They have an almost magical attachment to worrying. Unless events are approached with intense concern, the person feels that a disaster is likely. If your worry spiral feels as familiar as an old shoe, do not forget it is causing bodily damage. In fact, as you learn to use the strategies in this book, you may feel like you have lost a limb or that disaster will follow.

Chapter Three
Stopping the Worry Spiral: An Overview

"*F*inding temporary and specific causes for misfortune is the art of hope.... Finding permanent and universal causes for misfortune is the practice of despair."

–M. E. P. Seligman

Stopping the worry spiral involves a "return to nature." Nature provides a mechanism for reducing fear and anxiety. Briefly stated, the process of worry reduction occurs when you face a worry head-on, but in a way that the fear does not overwhelm you. Ordinarily fear and other emotions work to your advantage. Feelings give critical information about the environment that allows you to change the "cruise-control," or automatic pilot that regulates moment-to-moment acts. You do not have to think when you meet the grizzly bear in the woods. Emotions are hard-wired to the brain to make you run instantly. Without feelings you would plod along, slowly using reason to size up the situation. "Large brown object, alive, furry moving quickly toward me." If our forebears had to go through this laborious process to escape danger, human life in this state of nature would truly have been "nasty, brutish, and short."

Emotions, therefore, are nature's way to get your attention. Feelings linger because powerful chemicals surge and dissolve slowly. If the brain continues to focus on the danger, the body continues to manufacture the chemicals which translate into feeling fear. One strategy to stopping worry, then, is to train yourself to turn down this inner dialogue that keeps you focusing on the source of your fear.

Since you need to get on with life, the body also has a mechanism for reducing emotions once activated. The central nervous system (brain) has an inner principle that I call **biological boredom**. This principle operates constantly to keep you from being hypersensitive to outside stimulation. For example, if a jackhammer starts tearing up the street outside your room, you will react with a startle to the loud noise. Your nervous system is built so that it reacts to environmental changes. Gradually the jackhammer becomes background noise as you go about your business. Stimulation that repeats over and over causes boredom in the nervous system, and results in a weaker reaction.

This principle of biological boredom has a technical term in psychology. It is called *habituation* from the Latin word meaning to become accustomed to something. It works for all physical sensations such as sound, touch, vision, but operates for feelings as well. The human condition is such that any experience begins to change itself immediately. As the ancient philosopher said, "You cannot step twice into the same river."

You, no doubt, have experienced this law first-hand when you encountered grief or loss. When separated from a loved one, at first the pain is searing and almost unbearable. Mementoes of the person—a picture, a song, a favorite place—trigger intense sadness, and perhaps tears. Over time these same reminders lose their intensity, and looking at them causes less pain. Although it may sound cold, this represents the healing process that nature provides so that you can get on with your life. Without it you would remain frozen in grief. Psychologists call this gift of nature, this form of habituation, *emotional processing*. Emotional processing means that the intensity of a given emotional experience gradually lessens.

Emotional processing also works with anxiety and fear. Just as you overcome grief by facing the reminders of your loss so, too, you overcome anxiety associated with worry by facing its source. You need to stare down the worry, look it in the eye until your nervous system gets bored. We will discuss this strategy in more detail in Chapter Six under the name of exposure.

Dealing with worries also requires the gift of wisdom or discernment. Most worries boil down to one of two types. One set requires action to cope. These problems require you to seek information, generate alternative solutions, select a solution, implement it, and then evaluate its effect. Daily life abounds with such problems: a car that is not working, a job that provides too little income, a relationship that is distant, eyeglasses causing fuzzy vision, a pain in the back.

A second type of worry occurs when either a) all action plans have failed, or b) action plans will not take away the problem itself, even if they alleviate it. This includes chronic illness, inevitable loss, one-sided relationships, and systems too complex to change easily (e.g., income tax laws and government waste).

What makes this division tricky is that we cannot always know in advance the impact of taking action against a problem. The action of a single person or group sometimes can alter problems with overwhelming odds. In the 1960s a single, unsalaried attorney took on General Motors, then the United States' largest corporation, and influenced Congress to change auto safety legislation. Most of us, however, do not have Ralph Nader's skill or circumstances to devote our lives to mobilizing the public.

At the same time, people often give up on problems that seem beyond their control, but really are not. One person will attain full recovery from an orthopedic problem because he or she adheres to a strict exercise regimen; another does not, believing it will have no impact. One person remains open to a relationship that has cooled down by keeping up routine contact; another simply gives up.

Several years ago, when doing research on stress, I came to the last pages of the last book I had promised myself I would read on the topic. The author, a psychologist with no theological background to my knowledge, stated that all the literature on coping with stress could be summed up in the Serenity Prayer. "God, grant me the serenity to accept the things I cannot change; the courage to change the things I can; and the wisdom to know the difference." The remaining chapters, then, will explore the terrain of wisdom in change: how to assess a worry and determine which strategy to apply.

Chapter Four

Know Thyself: Naming the Fear

"*That which I fear most is fear.*"
—*Montaigne*

The ancient Greeks viewed wisdom from a different perspective than does a modern religious person. Yet they, too, saw self-knowledge as the first step in gaining virtue. As Plato noted, "The unexamined life is not worth living." Biblical writers observe that our modern emphasis on self-understanding or self-knowledge has no exact parallel in either the Hebrew or Christian scriptures. Self-understanding comes from facing God, from knowing the Creator, and it is in this encounter that we discover who we are.

Worry is fueled by avoidance. You fail to face your fear and this intensifies it. When you worry, despite your preoccupation, you actually work hard at not seeing. In the description of the earliest humans in Genesis, Adam hid after he sinned. He ran from the self-knowledge and self-understanding that would come from encountering God. In short, he was as much afraid of seeing himself as he was of seeing God.

This running and avoidance is not a conscious act. If you are feeling guilty or simply scared of the unknown, fear is instinctive and powerful. Psychological research reveals that you can literally turn off your perceptual tools when afraid, so that incoming threats do not even register in your brain. But even if the fear does not register in your awareness, it affects your body: heart rate, blood pressure, hormonal systems—all will activate. You will feel restless and upset, but not know the cause.

Self-understanding, then, is essential to coping with worry. Labeling or naming has the potential to confine or liberate. The revelation of God's name became a defining feature of Judaism. Jesus cast out demons by naming them. Labels, however, can also restrict. If you define yourself as "unimaginative," this category will create boundaries and expectations. You will act unimaginatively, thus creating your own negative reality.

Naming, however, brings relief from fear of the unknown. People with chronic, undiagnosed physical symptoms achieve a measure of peace when an expert finally diagnoses the ailment. You may have observed this even for cases which have no cure. People with emotional problems often feel relief when their condition is given a name. They feel liberated from viewing themselves as odd or "crazy." Similarly, naming your worries is more liberating than restricting.

To reduce your worries, however, requires more than just naming them. Coping requires an analysis of your worries to understand their full impact. I suggest that you self-observe your worries on a daily basis in the beginning. Figure 4-1 provides a simple form to record various aspects of worrying. You will need to identify the *content* or theme of your worry, its *intensity*, *how much time* you spend worrying, and *negative statements* that go through your mind when your worry. Figures 4-2 and 4-3 are sample records kept by John and Mary. John spends a good deal of time worrying about his financial situation. Mary cannot control thoughts about her married daughter. Each has negative thoughts that intensify his or her worrying, yet the thought of each is unique. John worries about the embarrassment of having creditors call about late bills. Mary cannot stop thinking about how unhappy her daughter is in her marriage.

The chief benefit to keeping a worry record is that you develop the habit of paying attention to your reactions. This attention is essential to reducing or eliminating excessive worrying. You could keep the record in your pocket or purse and make a note several times a day at some natural break (e.g., mealtime, freshening-up). Or, you might keep the record next to your bed and fill it out before retiring. Whatever works for you is best.

The next step after naming the worry is developing the *motivation* to stop worrying. The notion that you might be reluctant to give up your worries may seem ridiculous. Yet worrying may bring you a degree of comfort. You may believe that worrying *prevents some future disaster*. If you believe this, then not worrying feels unnatural. Or, you may appreciate that facing your worry means to give up the "benefits" of procrastination and avoidance. After all, one of the advantages to spinning your wheels is that you rarely move forward to face your fear head-on.

To develop the motivation to change, take a look at both the **benefits of giving up worrying and the costs of worrying**. Figure 4-4 provides one format for listing the benefits and costs. George listed his own costs and benefits in Figure 4-5. The benefits for him include reduced anxiety, increased concentration, better work performance, improved health, and having a serene mind. His costs include irritability and loss of temper, inability to enjoy the present moment, tension headaches, stomach upset, sleep disturbance, and mistakes due to being distracted.

Copy the blank Figure 4-4 (Personal Motivation List) and make your own cost/benefit list for your worries. The list will make clear what you may know intuitively or unconsciously. Do not be surprised if you find yourself resisting the very idea of looking at these costs and benefits. This act of assessing the worry damage takes courage, and may generate anxiety in itself. Yet you need to take this

risk, if only to see how it is in your self-interest to stop worrying. As Montaigne notes, "That which I fear most is fear," an idea Franklin Roosevelt used to galvanize a frightened nation during its worst economic depression. Making this list and keeping the worry record may represent your first steps in this ultimately spiritual journey. For, "To get into the core of God at his greatest, one must first get into the core of himself at his least; for no one can know God who has not first known himself" (Meister Eckhart).

Having named your worries and examined the many benefits of change, you are now ready for direct change strategies. Keep your Personal Motivation List handy for encouragement as you try the change strategies suggested later.

Figure 4-1
Daily Worry Record

Day	Situation	Worry Theme	Tension Level* 1–10	Time Spent Worrying	Thoughts you have about the Worry

*Tension Level:
  0 - 1 = No worry
  2 - 3 = Mild worry
  4 - 5 = Moderate worry
  6 - 7 = Severe worry
  8 - 10 = Intense worry

Figure 4-2
Daily Worry Record
(John's Record)

Day	Situation	Worry Theme	Tension Level* 1–10	Time Spent Worrying	Thoughts you have about the Worry
Mon.	Paying bills	Finances	7	2 hrs.	"How can I find money for my son's college books?"
Tues.	Trying to get to sleep	Finances	6	45 mins.	"What if the health insurance does not reimburse my dental surgery?"
Thurs.	At work— invited to join lunch group	Finances	4	20 mins.	"Should I accept the invitation to go to lunch with office colleagues? I didn't budget for it."

*Tension Level:
  0 - 1 = No worry
  2 - 3 = Mild worry
  4 - 5 = Moderate worry
  6 - 7 = Severe worry
 8 - 10 = Intense worry

Figure 4-3
Daily Worry Record
(Mary's Record)

Day	Situation	Worry Theme	Tension Level* 1–10	Time Spent Worrying	Thoughts you have about the Worry
Sat.	Daughter calls to arrange visit	Daughter's bad marriage	6	45 mins.	"She deserves better. He doesn't treat her right. She should get out of it."
Sun.	Daughter visiting with child	Daughter's bad marriage	8	3 hrs.	"What can she do? She has no job. She's dependent on him. She can't leave because the child's in a special school. He verbally abuses her."

*Tension Level:
  0 - 1 = No worry
  2 - 3 = Mild worry
  4 - 5 = Moderate worry
  6 - 7 = Severe worry
  8 - 10 = Intense worry

Figure 4-4
Personal Motivation List

Benefits of eliminating worry	1.
	2.
	3.
	4.
	5.
	6.
	7.
	8.
	9.
	10.
Cost of worrying	1.
	2.
	3.
	4.
	5.
	6.
	7.
	8.
	9.
	10.

Figure 4-5
Personal Motivation List
(George's Record)

Benefits of eliminating worry	1. Reduce anxiety
	2. Better concentration
	3. Better health
	4. Serene mind
	5.
	6.
	7.
	8.
	9.
	10.
Cost of worrying	1. Irritability
	2. Can't enjoy the present moment
	3. Tension headaches
	4. Upset stomach
	5. Can't sleep
	6. Mistakes at work from distractions
	7.
	8.
	9.
	10.

Chapter Five

Step One: Lowering the Volume

C*hapter Three gave an overview of the change process indicating that the first step requires lowering the volume of worrying. This means reducing the mind's inner dialogue, that noisy self-talk that fuels anxiety.*

Psychologists have found that two types of ideas fuel the bulk of this noise. The first *exaggerates* or *overpredicts* the possibility of a negative outcome. If you are worried about your work performance, speaking before a committee, or giving a presentation, your anxiety increases when you focus on the potential negative outcomes. You might reason, "What if they do not like my proposal? What

ances, not to rely on self. If vision is the perceptual mode of the first stage of religious experience, then *hearing* represents the second stage. What word, or sacred tradition speaks to you and challenges you to see God as beyond your present experience?

Finally, most religious experience carries with it a social dimension. Seeing and hearing God is not enough. I must enact through my conduct the vision and word that I experience. *Action and change* are essential components in genuine spirituality. Self-change is both personal and public; directed toward my interior attitude and my social behavior.

In my tradition this dimension is symbolized in Christ's resurrection, through which God begins to bring the world to completion and in which I must participate. I must participate by responding to God's help in changing myself and the world I live in. To what action does your own religious/spiritual tradition call you?

If you apply this model to the problem of worry, you have a method, if you choose, to integrate anxiety within your spirituality. I have pointed out three major traps triggering excessive worry. They include: 1) overpredicting the probability of negative events; 2) catastrophizing about your ability to cope with a negative event, if it occurs; and 3) avoiding the worry.

You can relate each trap to one part in the spiritual model. Each trap is a failure to trust one aspect of the full faith experience. Overpredicting is an inability *to see*, a failure to trust in the vision of God's presence.

When you fall victim to this trap, your vision focuses only on the negative aspects of reality. Catastrophizing is an inability *to listen*, a failure to trust the message that God is beyond and can deliver us from any event. Finally, avoiding what you worry about is a failure *to act*, not trusting in God's power to change you, not risking making God present in yourself and your world.

This outline requires a return to the Serenity Prayer. "God, grant me the serenity to accept the things I cannot change." Serenity is the mode of accepting God as beyond. Acceptance helps you avoid catastrophizing because you hear and believe, "My grace is sufficient for you." You have heard God's word enter history and select you to share divine life, unworthy though you feel. Serenity allows you to accept what you cannot change because belief in God-as-beyond convinces you how God has empowered you with unimaginable strength.

"The courage to change the things I can." Courage in the face of anxiety requires 1) self-exposure to your worries and fears; and 2) action plans to implement effective problem-solving. The paralysis created by your worries prevents you from fully realizing God's healing within you and for that portion of history entrusted to you.

"And the wisdom to know the difference." Wisdom comes from vision, from seeing the manifestations, the epiphanies, the presence of God. Wisdom in the personal sense comes first through self-awareness and self-knowledge. Through self-awareness you will know

God-as-present within yourself, through relationships, and in creation. According to David Tracy, "Every human understanding of God is at the same time an understanding of oneself—and vice versa." If you monitor your worries closely, you will discover your own nay-saying, your own denial of God's presence. You will startle yourself at your own negativity, at your own lack of vision, of how often you miss the manifestations. You will learn how you tend to overpredict the worst, as if God is not-with-us.

Although I have provided several guides for record keeping, you may find Figure 8-1 helpful, for it incorporates this spiritual model. When you track your worry or anxiety, reflect on how it fits into the overall framework. Ask yourself the question, "What is missing in my perspective?" What are you overpredicting and how do you need to become aware of God's presence in the event? How are you catastrophizing and what will help you see God as powerful, beyond human experience? How are you avoiding necessary action and what will encourage you to trust in God's power to change you and your world?

The universal wisdom of the Serenity Prayer's perspective repeats itself with each generation. We see it in the recent work of our poet laureate Maya Angelou: "What you're supposed to do when you don't like a thing is change it. If you can't change it, change the way you think about it."

The psychological paradox means that facing fear

results not in danger but freedom. The theological paradox is a larger metaphor for this process. Instead of hiding from God, as did Adam and Eve, staying with our fear of the Lord gives perspective to who we are. If we try to stand fast and face this fear, rather than destroying us, we find that "perfect love casts out fear."

Figure 8-1
Worry and Serenity

1. Worry: _____

_____

_____

Hearing	Enacting	Seeing
God's Judgment	God's Call	God's Presence
ACCEPTANCE	ABILITY TO CHANGE	WISDOM

1. What is it about this worry problem that can *not* change?	1. What about this worry problem *can* I change?	1. What *positives* am I failing to see in this worry?
2. How does its unchangeablility fit in with my need for God's grace or favor?	2. How is God calling me to enact my faith in the world?	2. Where is God's presence for me in this worry?

1. _____ 1. _____ 1. _____

_____

_____

_____

2. _____ 2. _____ 2. _____

_____

_____

_____

Further Reading

The books recommended below were written for the general public and are based on cognitive and behavioral strategies for reducing anxiety and worry. All are in paperback.

Living with Fear. By Isaac Marks, M.D. McGraw-Hill, 1978.

Mastery of Your Anxiety and Worry. By Michelle Craske, Ph.D, David Barlow, Ph.D., and Tracy O'Leary. Graywind Publications, 1992.

Mastering Stress: A Lifestyle Approach. By David Barlow, Ph.D., and Ronald Rapee, Ph.D. American Health Publishing Co., 1991.

Other Books in the Series

Little Pieces of Light...Darkness and Personal Growth
by Joyce Rupp

Lessons from the Monastery That Touch Your Life
by M. Basil Pennington, O.C.S.O.

As You and the Abused Person Journey Together
by Sharon E. Cheston

Spirituality, Stress & You
by Thomas E. Rodgerson

Joy, The Dancing Spirit of Love Surrounding You
by Beverly Elaine Eanes

Every Decision You Make Is a Spiritual One
by Anthony J. De Conciliis with John F. Kinsella

Celebrating the Woman You Are
by S. Suzanne Mayer, IHM